D0251575

IF GOD WILL PROVIDE, WHY DO WE HAVE TO ASK FOR MONEY?

Rick Dunham

Published by Dunham Books
© 2007 by Rick Dunham and Dunham+Company
Published 2007
Second Printing
ISBN: 978-1-934590-16-4

Unless otherwise indicated, Scripture verses quoted are
taken with permission from the New International Version.

Cover design by: Michael Holter Creative

For more information:

Dunham
books

15455 Dallas Parkway, Sixth Floor
Addison, TX 75001
dunhambooks.com

CONTENTS

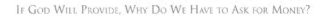

FOREWORD

Having been involved in Christian ministry for over 25 years, one of the most significant and relentless challenges I have faced is developing the financial support for those ministries. More often than not, it has been a genuine struggle!

Now, if we're honest, as leaders we see fundraising as a necessary evil. We wish we could just have the money somehow appear so we could focus on what we care about most… doing the ministry God has called us to do!

I think we've missed the point.

As this book makes abundantly clear, our work in developing the funds for our ministries is in fact a vital part of our ministry! It has significant spiritual implications not only for your ministry, but for those who support your ministry.

If God Will Provide, Why Do We Have to Ask for Money? is a truly fresh and thoroughly biblical perspective on our mandate as leaders to challenge God's people to fund His work in the world today. Whether you are a church leader, the head of a non-profit ministry, or a donor to either, I believe you will find this book a challenge to your view of giving.

I pray as you open this book, you will also open your mind and heart to allow God to speak to you through my good friend, Rick Dunham. As a Christian leader, may you be challenged about your responsibility to engage and motivate God's people to generously support His Kingdom work. And as a child of God, may you come to understand why your responsibility to financially support God's work is so important to His Kingdom program… and to your spiritual walk.

Chip Ingram
President,
Living on the Edge

INTRODUCTION

The scene was perfectly set. After months of planning, we had brought together some of our organization's most important supporters. As I recall, it was one of our first events designed to build a deeper relationship with current and potential major donors.

Finally! It was exciting to think we were taking this important step to deepen these critical relationships.

Then the president rose and addressed the gathering.

"I have finally figured out what the president of a charitable organization does. He lives in a big house and begs."

AUGGHH!! I could have died! While I was

concerned about what this said to our donors, I was more concerned about what this said about our president's view of fundraising. It was clear he viewed fundraising as begging people to part with their money.

Fundraising was a necessary evil at best.

Perhaps you feel that way, too. Or perhaps you feel like the donor who sent the following note to a ministry I was once working with,

> *If the Lord has truly called you to this ministry, He will supply all your needs according to His riches in glory by Christ Jesus. And if God has truly called you to ministry, He will assuredly supply all of your needs including the financial ones without you doing the fundraising.*

If we are honest, all of us involved in fundraising—whether in the local church or a Christian ministry—have at some time or another had similar thoughts. When it comes to raising money to fund our ministry, most of us have felt a range of emotions—from being uncomfortable with asking people for money, to perhaps even being embarrassed. For some leaders, it feels inappropriate to ask people to part with their hard-earned money. And for others, it does feel like begging.

Yet, as Christian leaders who are responsible for raising money for ministry, there are some critical questions we have to ask:

- Does asking for money honor God?
- Is it something that He sanctions and blesses?
- How important is fundraising to God?
- If it is important, why?

I believe a careful study of Scripture shows that God not only sanctions fundraising, it's His expectation. Yes, He expects Christian leaders to challenge His people to fund His Kingdom work here on earth. In fact, I would go so far as to say that this is His mandate. But not for the reasons you or I might think.

In the following pages, I want to unpack those reasons for you. I want to show you why I believe raising money for ministry is an issue at the very center of both the spiritual walk of each Christian and the work of the Church in our world today. My prayer is that you will open your heart and mind to allow the truth of Scripture to inform and perhaps even rebuild your view of fundraising... and of giving... to support God's work.

If you are responsible for raising money for your church or organization, I pray that you will be freed and energized to engage Christians to financially support what God is doing to impact people's lives through your ministry today. And if you are reading this as a supporter of God's work, I pray you will come to understand just how crucial your generous giving is to God's Kingdom work and to your spiritual vitality.

The Spiritual Dynamics of Fundraising

CHAPTER ONE

THE REALITY OF THE BATTLE

To understand what is at stake in the funding of Christian ministry—and why the issue of fundraising is such a crucial issue for ministry—it's vital you and I understand the spiritual dynamic that is at play when we talk about funding Christian ministry.

That dynamic is the spiritual war in which we find ourselves.

This spiritual war is in actuality the framework that informs the entirety of our lives today. It is not just some sideline theological teaching as most Christians believe it is. In fact, it's something I believe we in the western world don't fully understand or appreciate, which is why so many Christians live in a state of constant spiritual defeat.

But this war is real. Very real.

In his book, *Waking the Dead*, John Eldredge makes a simple but powerful statement: "Things are not what they seem. This is a world at war."

He then goes on to explain,

> *The world in which we live is a combat zone, a violent clash of kingdoms, a bitter struggle unto the death. ...You were born into a world at war, and you will live all your days in the midst of a great battle, involving all the forces of heaven and hell and played out here on earth.... Until we come to terms with war as the context of our days, we will not understand life (pp. 13, 17).*

I believe most Christians today would give an assenting nod to the notion of spiritual warfare. But in fact, the reality of spiritual conflict does not inform how the vast majority of Christians in the western world live.

And I think that's true of Christian leaders as well—especially in how they lead Christian ministries. They often fail to see their work and the work of their ministry or church in light of the epic spiritual battle going on all around us.

Eldredge goes on to quote C.S. Lewis, when he wrote in *Mere Christianity*,

> *One of the things that surprised me when I first read the New Testament seriously was that it talked so much about a Dark Power in the universe—a mighty evil spirit who was held to be the Power behind death and disease and sin....*
>
> *This universe is at war.*

OVER AND OVER AGAIN, THE BIBLICAL RECORD ALLOWS US A GLIMPSE OF THIS WAR BY PULLING BACK THE CURTAIN ON OUR PHYSICAL WORLD.

Over and over again, the biblical record allows us a glimpse of this war by pulling back the curtain on our physical world. Scripture is replete with examples that, frankly, have become too familiar.

The Battle Engaged

The battle against Satan and his forces of evil was the focal point of Jesus' ministry. In fact, the Bible tells us that defeating Satan was the purpose Jesus came to earth. As John states in 1 John 3:8,

> *The reason the Son of God appeared was to destroy the devil's work.*

THE LIFE OF JESUS WAS DEFINED BY THE EPIC WAR BEING WAGED BY THE FORCES OF DARKNESS AGAINST GOD AND HIS PLAN TO REDEEM MANKIND.

The life of Jesus was defined by the epic war being waged by the forces of darkness against God and His plan to redeem mankind. And it culminated in His seeming defeat on the cross… and His stunning victory when He rose from the dead.

We see this battle played out in the life of Christ in so many ways. But perhaps the greatest evidence of this war was the temptation of Christ.

When we read the account of how Christ was tempted by Satan in the wilderness, we tend to sanitize the event by thinking of it as a debate between Jesus and the devil. No. It was a hand-to-hand spiritual fight! The stakes were the future of all mankind… and the fulfillment of God's Kingdom program hung in the balance.

Have you ever noticed that after Satan tempted Jesus by asking Him to turn a stone into bread—to make Jesus break His 40-day fast—that he then "took" Jesus to the highest point of the temple… and to a high mountain?

Do you think it was not a fight? Certainly Jesus, as all-powerful God, allowed this battle to take place. But nevertheless, it was a battle. If it wasn't, why did the angels need to come and attend to Jesus after Satan finally left Him?

No, the temptation of Christ wasn't a sideshow. It was the main attraction—the battle between the forces of good and evil… between darkness and light… that have been at odds since the moment

Satan rebelled.

Even the Old Testament gives evidence of this hidden, ongoing battle. Take, for example, the scene as described in Daniel chapter 10. It's an incredibly fascinating passage that gives us a glimpse into the spiritual realm and the battle that is constantly being waged.

Here is what an angel tells Daniel in response to his prayer,

> *"Since the first day that you set your mind to gain understanding and to humble yourself before your God, your words were heard, and I have come in response to them. But the prince of the Persian kingdom resisted me twenty-one days. Then Michael, one of the chief princes, came to help me, because I was detained there with the king of Persia" (vv. 12-13).*

The forces of evil stood against the angel sent from God. They fought ferociously to keep the angel away from Daniel for 21 days. In fact, it took the help of Michael, the archangel, for the angel sent by God to finally be victorious over the demonic "prince of the Persian kingdom."

There are indeed spiritual forces of evil at work doing all they can to thwart God's purposes and to hamper His Kingdom program.

Then there is the following passage in Revelation chapter 12 that is immensely revealing,

> *A great and wondrous sign appeared in heaven: a woman clothed with the sun, with the moon under her feet and a crown of twelve stars on her head. She was pregnant and cried out in pain as she was about to give birth. Then another sign appeared in heaven: an enormous red dragon with seven heads and ten horns and seven crowns on his heads.... The dragon stood in front of the woman who was about to give birth, so that he might devour her child the moment it was born. She gave birth to a son, a male child, who will rule all the nations with an iron scepter....*

And there was war in heaven. Michael and his angels fought against the dragon, and the dragon and his angels fought back. But he was not strong enough, and they lost their place in heaven.

Then the dragon was enraged at the woman and went off to make war against the rest of her offspring—those who obey God's commandments and hold to the testimony of Jesus (vv. 1-5, 7-8, 17).

Satan, the dragon, is an avowed enemy of Jesus. He has done… is doing… and will do… anything he can to thwart God's purposes.

The Battle Continues

Even though Satan was defeated when Christ rose from the dead, for him the battle continues. He is committed to destroying the offspring of Jesus… that's you and me! Which is why Jesus said what He did to Paul on the road to Damascus.

In Acts 26, we have the record of that conversation in Paul's eloquent defense of his faith before King Agrippa. As he addresses the king, he recounts his dramatic conversion on the road to Damascus where he came face to face with the resurrected Christ. And he repeats what Jesus told him his purpose would be from that day forward.

Jesus told Paul...

> EVEN THOUGH SATAN WAS DEFEATED WHEN CHRIST ROSE FROM THE DEAD, FOR HIM THE BATTLE CONTINUES.

"... I am sending you to them to open their eyes and turn them from darkness to light, and from the power of Satan to God, so that they may receive forgiveness of sins and a place among those who are sanctified by faith in me" (vv. 17-18).

Jesus made clear to Paul that his purpose would be defined by engaging the forces of darkness... to move people from the power and dominion of Satan to the power and dominion of God. And no matter what ministry you are involved with today, that is your purpose. God has called you to be part of His plan to free people from the power of Satan and his kingdom of darkness and bring them into God's Kingdom of light.

But don't think for a moment that Satan will not put up a fight! That's why Peter warns us in 1 Peter 5:8,

> *Be self-controlled and alert. Your enemy the devil prowls around like a roaring lion looking for someone to devour.*

And it's why Paul reminds us in Ephesians 6:10-12 that the true field of battle is in the spiritual realm,

> *Finally, be strong in the Lord and in His mighty power. Put on the full armor of God so that you can take your stand against the devil's schemes. For our struggle is not against flesh and blood, but against the rulers, against the authorities, against the powers of this dark world and against the spiritual forces of evil in the heavenly realms.*

We are players in a cosmic war. We must

understand that this is our reality… that this epic spiritual struggle continues in our world today.

Now, you may be wondering, "What in the world does this have to do with fundraising?" Everything!

Chapter Two

The Battle of Funding Christian Ministry

The spiritual war between Satan and his forces of darkness and God and His forces of light is at the core of God's Kingdom work here on earth. And it's being waged on a variety of fronts.

But there is one particular battlefront that is nearly always overlooked. It's a place where the forces of evil are enjoying victory after victory over God's children… to the detriment of God's Kingdom work.

> I BELIEVE THAT THE FUNDING OF GOD'S WORK IN THE WORLD TODAY IS A NEXUS—A FOCAL POINT.

This battlefront is the funding of Christian ministry. I believe that the funding of God's work in the world today is a nexus—a focal point—that is central, not tangential, to the fulfillment of God's purposes in our world today. This makes the funding of Christian ministry a prime target for Satan and the spiritual authorities under his command.

Because this is such a critical front in the spiritual battle, I believe there are two significant spiritual implications for God's Kingdom program today.

Limited Resources Means Limited Impact

The first implication is quite obvious: If a ministry is limited in funding, it… by definition… is limited in its impact.

Clearly, the ability of a ministry to fulfill God's call is in direct proportion to its ability to fund its work. And if the devil and his forces can thwart Christians from supporting God's work, then he has won a victory in undermining the advancement and impact of God's Kingdom here on earth.

On one of my trips to Australia, I had the opportunity to have a private breakfast with the former head of Australia's Special Forces, Jim Wallace. This gentleman served for over 35 years in the armed forces and taught at their elite military college for years.

As we were discussing this issue of the funding of Christian ministry and how it is one of the areas where the spiritual battle is fiercely engaged, Jim's eyes lit up. What he went on to share both stunned and energized me.

He explained that battles are not won based on tactics, but rather on destroying the resources of the enemy. In fact, he said that's one of the tasks of Special Forces… getting behind enemy lines and destroying the enemy's ability to supply the troops engaged in the battle.

If the enemy doesn't have fuel, bullets, food, medical supplies—all the necessary things to wage the battle—they can't fight. And they lose.

That is exactly Satan's strategy: ***to keep ministries from gaining the resources they need to do the work God has called them to do.*** If he can do that, ministries are limited in what they can do.

I have often asked ministry leaders what they would do if they had all the money they needed. Invariably, their eyes light up when they begin to recite the vision they would fulfill… if only they had the money!

HOW MANY OPPORTUNITIES HAVE BEEN MISSED… BECAUSE WE FAIL TO EFFECTIVELY FUND MINISTRY?

Unfortunately, this lack of funding is sometimes worn as a badge of honor by ministry leaders. The "poverty" of their ministry is transformed from a spiritual defeat—which it is—to somehow being an indication of just how spiritual they are as they "trust God" for His provision.

But my question then becomes, how many lives have not been transformed… how many hearts have not been won to Christ… how many opportunities have been missed… because we fail to effectively fund ministry?

As we will see, the responsibility to motivate God's people to fund God's work in the world

lies squarely on the shoulders of ministry leaders.
It is their responsibility to move God's people to
financially engage in what He is doing in the world.
It's a simple but thoroughly biblical principle: ***When
ministry leaders are called by God to do His work,
they are also called to challenge His people to fund
that work!***

Why? Is God unable to provide the resources?
Doesn't Psalm 50:10 tell us that God owns the cattle
on a thousand hills?

Absolutely! But, as we will see in this book, God
has chosen to fund His work on earth through His
people. And He's done so for one reason... and it's
not the money. He already owns that.

What God wants is the one thing you own and
have complete control over. Your heart.

The Battlefield of the Heart

God passionately desires the whole-hearted
devotion of every one of His children. The Bible is

clear that this is at the top of God's agenda.

In 2 Chronicles 16:9, we find one of the most incredible verses in the Bible. It was spoken by the prophet Hanani when he confronted King Asa for his lack of trust in God. In his rebuke, Hanani makes this powerful statement… an insightful glimpse into the passion and focus of God:

GOD PASSIONATELY DESIRES THE WHOLE-HEARTED DEVOTION OF EVERY ONE OF HIS CHILDREN.

"For the eyes of the LORD range throughout the earth to strengthen those whose hearts are fully committed to him."

God's priority and passion is to have those whose hearts are truly and totally His. In fact, this is really at the core of Jesus' statement in Mark 12:30,

"Love the Lord your God with all your heart and with all your soul and with all your mind and with all your strength."

God has no greater desire than to have your

whole heart!

God doesn't want to be a part of your life. He wants to *be* your life. He wants your total and complete devotion, and He wants to be the affection of your heart.

God places a priority on the heart because it is the place of spiritual transaction. We are told in Scripture that salvation comes because we believe in our heart (Romans 10:9) and that faith is a matter of the heart (Proverbs 3:5-6).

And the heart is the one common denominator of Christian ministry. Whether your ministry is a church, a Christian radio or television station, a media ministry, or is dedicated to relief and development or urban renewal, every ministry is ultimately focused on one thing: winning and growing the hearts of men, women and children so they become wholly devoted followers of Jesus Christ.

The heart is the battlefield of every Christian ministry. Winning people to Christ is a transaction of the heart. And at its core, the process of discipleship is growing people in their faith… to expand their heart for God so that God will ultimately own that entire real estate.

So how does this relate to fundraising? In two ways.

First, if we fail to properly fund Christian ministry, then we limit the ministry's ability to reach people to bring them into a personal relationship with God or grow them in the faith as disciples of Christ. Which means we suffer loss on the spiritual battlefront for the hearts of men and women.

That's one reason why, if you are a Christian leader, you must be bold in challenging God's people to fund His work. And it's why, as a follower of Christ, you must be serious in your commitment to funding God's Kingdom work… whether that's through your local church or a Christian ministry.

But there's a second implication. And this is the one I believe most ministries don't fully understand.

When we fail to properly engage Christians to fund God's Kingdom work, we fail to grow their whole-hearted devotion for God.

Jesus Himself made it abundantly clear that our money and our heart are inextricably tied together. How we view money… and what we do with money… have everything to do with whether God has our whole heart. And if having the whole heart of His children is God's deepest desire, then He cares a lot about how we use the money He has entrusted to us.

You and I cannot be wholly devoted to God if we are not investing in His Kingdom work with what He has put into our trust. Because our hearts follow wherever we invest our money!

So when we as God's people fund His work, God gets what He really wants—our whole-hearted devotion and commitment to Him.

And your whole-hearted devotion to God is the last thing Satan wants. So you can understand why he is so actively resisting and thwarting the funding of God's work here on earth. Satan not only wants to undermine God's Kingdom work by limiting the resources a ministry has to fund its work, he also wants to keep each believer from giving his or her whole heart and soul in service to God.

So fundraising… and the issue of giving… is indeed a critical part of the Christian life. Raising money for ministry is not really the practice of getting people to part with their hard-earned money. It's getting men and women to align their hearts with what God is doing in the world today and to increase the devotion of their hearts to Him by investing in what He is doing in the world. Because that's what giving is really all about!

So anyone involved in fundraising—or challenging God's people to give to God's Kingdom program—is really in the business of helping to align a person's heart with God's heart.

An honest review of Scripture shows there is indeed a clear biblical basis—even a mandate—for fundraising. Again, it's not focused primarily on money, but rather on what the giving of that money means for achieving God's goals of ministry impact… and the alignment of a person's heart with His heart.

GOD PLACES A PRIORITY ON THE HEART BECAUSE IT IS THE PLACE OF SPIRITUAL TRANSACTION.

There are three perspectives from God's Word which make that mandate clear. The first is the **biblical view of money**. The second is the **biblical view of giving**. And the third is the **biblical view of asking**. We'll unpack these three perspectives over the next few chapters.

As we do, I want you to think about this for a moment: If Satan can keep Christians from supporting God's work, he accomplishes his top two goals in one mighty swoop. Not only does he thwart the advancement of God's Kingdom, he keeps the heart of the believer from a whole-hearted commitment to Jesus Christ. What a brilliant strategy!

The stakes are immense. It's vital that we as Christian leaders understand the importance of this critical battlefront and determine not to let Satan have this victory! And as supporters of God's work, we all need to understand what Satan is really up to and why our investment in God's Kingdom must be a spiritual priority.

A Biblical Model
for Fundraising

CHAPTER THREE

THE BIBLICAL VIEW OF MONEY

The first piece of intelligence we need in this battle is to understand how God views money. In Ecclesiastes 5, Solomon gives us a good starting place.

As you probably know, Ecclesiastes is Solomon's record of how he tested and probed the facets of life to see what would bring genuine satisfaction. And one of the facets Solomon probed was wealth.

First, Solomon affirms that God is the One who blesses a person with wealth. In Ecclesiastes 5:19, he says,

> *Moreover, when God gives any man wealth and possessions, and enables him to enjoy them, to accept his lot and be happy in his work—this is a gift of God.*

God is the giver of wealth. Makes sense. If God owns it all, then it stands to reason that our wealth is just part of what God already owns.

This truth is a driving principle for David in 1 Chronicles 29:10-14,

> David praised the LORD in the presence of the whole assembly, saying, "Praise be to you, O LORD, God of our father Israel, from everlasting to everlasting.
>
> "Yours, O LORD, is the greatness and the power and the glory and the majesty and the splendor, for everything in heaven and earth is yours. Yours, O LORD, is the kingdom; you are exalted as head over all.
>
> "Wealth and honor come from you; you are the ruler of all things. In your hands are strength and power to exalt and give strength to all.
>
> "Now, our God, we give you thanks, and praise your glorious name.
>
> "But who am I, and who are my people, that

we should be able to give as generously as this?
Everything comes from you, and we have given
you only what comes from your hand."

God owns it all and any wealth that you or I
might acquire comes from God's own treasury!

But Solomon makes another point in that same
verse. God expects us to enjoy what He has given us.
When God gives wealth, He gives the power to enjoy
it. So whatever money we have, we need to see it as a
gift from God and not feel guilty
about what He's given us!

Finally, Solomon makes
clear that the person whose life
is driven by money will never
be satisfied because money can't
deliver ultimate satisfaction. He
says in Ecclesiastes 5:10-11,

> So whatever money we have, we need to see it as a gift from God and not feel guilty about what He's given us!

Whoever loves money
never has money enough;
whoever loves wealth is never satisfied with

his income. This too is meaningless. As goods increase, so do those who consume them. And what benefit are they to the owner except to feast his eyes on them?

God may give you wealth and the power to enjoy it, but you'll never be satisfied if your life is driven by the desire for wealth.

In these verses, Solomon tells us why money can't bring ultimate satisfaction. First, there's never enough. No matter how wealthy you are, there's never enough.

GOD WANTS US TO RECOGNIZE THAT MONEY IS TEMPORAL AND THAT OUR LIVES SHOULD NEVER BE DRIVEN BY ACCUMULATING IT.

The story goes that somebody once asked John D. Rockefeller how much money is enough. His response? "One dollar more!" We've all experienced that long-awaited raise only to wonder what happened to it after we paid the bills!

Second, money can't bring ultimate satisfaction because it's temporal. It's vanity to love wealth because money will ultimately disappear. If accumulating wealth is your sole or primary ambition in life, then you're driven by the temporal... not the eternal. And you'll never know true happiness or genuine satisfaction.

You know, I'm struck by how balanced Solomon is in this chapter of Ecclesiastes. On the one hand, he wants us to understand that whatever God does give, He empowers us to enjoy. But on the other hand, he wants us to recognize that money is temporal and that our lives should never be driven by accumulating it.

Treasuring the Right Treasures

Jesus also deals directly with the futility of a life driven by accumulating wealth. Here's what He says in Matthew 6:19-24,

> *"Do not store up for yourselves treasures on earth, where moth and rust destroy, and*

*where thieves break in and steal. But store up
for yourselves treasures in heaven, where moth
and rust do not destroy, and where thieves do not
break in and steal. For where your treasure is,
there your heart will be also.*

*"The eye is the lamp of the body. If your
eyes are good, your whole body will be full of
light. But if your eyes are bad, your whole body
will be full of darkness. If then the light within
you is darkness, how great is that darkness!*

*"No one can serve two masters. Either he
will hate the one and love the other, or he will
be devoted to the one and despise the other. You
cannot serve both God and Money."*

The first thing that hits me in this passage is the
recognition by Jesus that the accumulation of wealth
is a natural drive of the human heart. This is why
Christ uses the word *treasures* rather than *money*.

Treasures deal with the issues of the heart. And
God knows the degree to which we treasure money

is the degree to which it has captured our heart. For when our hearts "treasure up treasure" (that is the literal translation), then God cannot have our whole heart.

We *will* accumulate the stuff we treasure. The only question is where. If we accumulate the stuff of earth, it's temporary. If we accumulate the stuff of heaven, it's permanent and eternal—with implications that can only be measured on an infinite scale.

> GOD KNOWS THE DEGREE TO WHICH WE TREASURE MONEY IS THE DEGREE TO WHICH IT HAS CAPTURED OUR HEART.

And when that is our focus, God will have our whole heart, which is *His* greatest treasure!

Verses 22-23 of Matthew chapter 6 seem a little odd, don't you think? "The eye is the lamp of the body. If your eyes are good, your whole body will be full of light. But if your eyes are bad, your whole body will be full of darkness. If then the light within you is darkness, how great is that darkness!"

Here's the truth I think Christ is hammering home: *If you've got the wrong focus, you're in big trouble.* If the light, the thing you're focused on, the thing you think is right, is wrong, how terribly wrong you are!

So if your view of money is messed up... if your relationship with wealth and treasure is perverted... then your heart will be in the wrong place and the consequences will be devastating.

The Accountability of Stewardship

Christ elaborates on His view of money in Matthew 25:14-30. In this passage He takes a slightly different angle as He wants us to understand the accountability we will have as stewards of what He has entrusted to us.

> *"Again, it will be like a man going on a journey, who called his servants and entrusted his property to them. To one he gave five talents*

of money, to another two talents, and to another one talent, each according to his ability. Then he went on his journey. The man who had received the five talents went at once and put his money to work and gained five more. So also, the one with the two talents gained two more. But the man who had received the one talent went off, dug a hole in the ground and hid his master's money.

"After a long time the master of those servants returned and settled accounts with them. The man who had received the five talents brought the other five. 'Master,' he said, 'you entrusted me with five talents. See, I have gained five more.'

"His master replied, 'Well done, good and faithful servant! You have been faithful with a few things; I will put you in charge of many things. Come and share your master's happiness!'

"The man with the two talents also came. 'Master,' he said, 'you entrusted me with two

talents; see, I have gained two more.'

"His master replied, 'Well done, good and faithful servant! You have been faithful with a few things; I will put you in charge of many things. Come and share your master's happiness!'

"Then the man who had received the one talent came. 'Master,' he said, 'I knew that you are a hard man, harvesting where you have not sown and gathering where you have not scattered seed. So I was afraid and went out and hid your talent in the ground. See, here is what belongs to you.'

"His master replied, 'You wicked, lazy servant! So you knew that I harvest where I have not sown and gather where I have not scattered seed? Well then, you should have put my money on deposit with the bankers, so that when I returned I would have received it back with interest.

"'Take the talent from him and give it to the one who has the ten talents. For everyone who has will be given more, and he will have an abundance. Whoever does not have, even what he has will be taken from him. And throw that worthless servant outside, into the darkness, where there will be weeping and gnashing of teeth.'"

"WELL DONE, GOOD AND FAITHFUL SERVANT! YOU HAVE BEEN FAITHFUL WITH A FEW THINGS; I WILL PUT YOU IN CHARGE OF MANY THINGS."

Jesus' point? God views money as a stewardship. God entrusts His resources to His people based on their capacity to handle those resources, He expects them to effectively invest those resources for maximum return, and He will ultimately hold them accountable.

Think for a moment about those who support your ministry. God has given them resources that are His—and His decision to entrust those resources to them is based on their ability to handle those resources. He fully expects them to invest their resources wisely in His Kingdom work.

And as a supporter of God's Kingdom work, God cares passionately about how you utilize what He has entrusted to you. He will hold you accountable for how you invest what He has given you. But remember, you also have been given the ability to effectively invest what He has given you in His work.

As we saw earlier, those who invest in God's Kingdom work will lay up eternal treasure, which means that's where their heart will be. And that is God's ultimate desire. But those who fail to effectively invest in God's Kingdom work will never become wholly devoted followers of God because their hearts will be devoted to the temporal, which will someday fade away.

That's why it's critical that you see the funding of your ministry as an important spiritual goal… if indeed God has called your ministry into being.

Because when donors invest in your ministry, they are doing what God wants them to do—that is, providing the funding of His work here on earth and laying up treasures in heaven, investing for maximum eternal return. And God is getting what He wants… their hearts!

CHAPTER FOUR

THE BIBLICAL VIEW OF GIVING

Now that we have an idea of how God views money and the importance of stewardship, it's vital we understand how God views giving. This is the second piece of critical intelligence in this battle of funding God's Kingdom work.

The first passage that helps us understand how God views giving is Exodus 25:1-2. In this passage, Moses is on Mount Sinai. He is in the presence of the Lord to receive the Ten Commandments. The first words out of God's mouth are incredibly telling,

> *"Tell the Israelites to bring me an offering. You are to receive the offering for me from each man whose heart prompts him to give."*

Wow! In the midst of giving the Ten Commandments—one of the greatest moments in history—God begins the conversation by telling Moses how important it is to Him that His people give an offering to Him out of their resources!

And notice that God immediately connects giving with the heart. God wants His people to give with a willing and properly motivated heart. Again, our heart and our money are inseparable.

God makes it clear that giving is really a matter of the heart. Why? When we willingly give money to God's work, we have mastery over money and it no longer has mastery over us. Our heart is given to where we have put it… into God's Kingdom work.

But when we hoard money, it owns us and our heart, not allowing God to own that most important real estate.

So in obedience, Moses gathers the people together and challenges them to give an offering to God. It's documented in Exodus 35, where we find the people joyfully giving with their whole hearts!

So in the second book of the Bible, when God's Kingdom program here on earth (the building of the tabernacle) needs funding, God establishes a precedent—a principle: ***His people are to give of their resources to make His plan to impact the world possible.***

This truth is reinforced in 1 Chronicles 29. In this chapter, David raises up contributions for the building of the temple. Verse 9 states,

WHEN WE WILLINGLY GIVE MONEY TO GOD'S WORK, WE HAVE MASTERY OVER MONEY. IT NO LONGER HAS MASTERY OVER US.

> *The people rejoiced at the willing response of their leaders, for they had given freely and wholeheartedly to the LORD. David the king also rejoiced greatly.*

And then David prays the following prayer just a few verses later in verse 17,

> *"I know, my God, that you test the heart and are pleased with integrity. All these things have I given willingly and with honest intent. And now I have seen with joy how willingly your people, who are here, have given to you."*

God expects His people to fund His work here on earth. And when they give, it is always a matter of the heart.

The Priority of Giving

Another passage to help us understand God's view on giving is 2 Corinthians 8. But to properly understand this chapter, you need to understand its context.

GOD EXPECTS HIS PEOPLE TO FUND HIS WORK HERE ON EARTH.

The Corinthian church was very wealthy, but it struggled to live as God desired. One might go so far as to say it was the misfit of the early Church. In 2 Corinthians 8, Paul is forced to get in the face of the Corinthians for not fulfilling a promise they had made to support the suffering church in Jerusalem.

So Paul begins to put the pressure on the Corinthian church when he talks to them about the churches in Macedonia. This is what he says in verses 1-4,

> *And now, brothers, we want you to know about the grace that God has given the Macedonia churches. Out of the most severe trial, their overflowing joy and their extreme poverty welled up in rich generosity. For I testify that they gave as much as they were able, and even beyond their ability. Entirely on their own they urgently pleaded with us for the privilege of sharing in this service to the saints.*

To understand the power of this statement, you need to understand that the Macedonian church was, in fact, *extremely* poor. Yet, in contrast to the wealthy Corinthian church, they had more than fulfilled their own commitment.

But Paul really delivers a hard message in verse 5 when he goes on to say, "And they did not do as we expected, but they gave themselves first to the Lord and then to us in keeping with God's will."

Ouch! That had to sting the leaders of the Corinthian church!! But I believe Paul was so strong with them because he wanted the Corinthians to understand that giving was to be a priority because it was a clear indication of whether God had their heart and their genuine devotion.

Don't miss this powerful principle: ***Our giving is evidence of whether or not we have truly given ourselves to God.*** You can't skate around that one. In fact, let me put it this way. A non-giving follower of Christ is an oxymoron. You can't proclaim to be following Christ and not invest in His Kingdom work to push back the spiritual darkness of Satan's kingdom!

Forgive me, but this is such a huge issue in the Church today, I'm going to camp here a bit and preach.

The reality facing the Church and Christian ministries today is that most Christians are ignorant when it comes to understanding the vital spiritual importance of giving. If you are a pastor, I want to challenge you to love your people enough to teach them the biblical truth about giving. If your heart's desire is to see your people become wholly devoted followers of Christ, then you can't ignore this issue! You owe it to them to help them build a biblical understanding of how giving and following Christ are inextricably linked.

IF YOU ARE A PASTOR, I WANT TO CHALLENGE YOU TO LOVE YOUR PEOPLE ENOUGH TO TEACH THEM THE BIBLICAL TRUTH ABOUT GIVING.

It may be uncomfortable, but it is part of the whole counsel of God… and it is one of our Lord's major priorities. So it should be one of yours, too.

Remember, it is the spiritual transaction of the heart that God cares about more than the financial transaction itself.

The Blessing of Giving

Finally, we need to understand that biblical giving results in blessing to those who give. Nowhere in the Bible is this clearer than in the book of Philippians.

One of the reasons Paul wrote Philippians was to thank the Christians in Philippi for all they had done to encourage him in his ministry and his work. This included their consistent financial support of him.

In Philippians 4:17, he says,

> *Not that I am looking for a gift, but I am looking for what may be credited to your account.*

Paul understood Christ's teaching about the proper investment of a person's treasure. If a person's investment is in Kingdom work, it accrues to the benefit of the giver by compounding for eternity. Now that's some investment! And that is some blessing!

Paul also addresses the blessings that flow from giving in 2 Corinthians 9:6-11. In this passage he tells us,

> *Remember this: Whoever sows sparingly will also reap sparingly, and whoever sows generously will also reap generously. Each man should give what he has decided in his heart*

*to give, not reluctantly or under compulsion,
for God loves a cheerful giver. And God is able
to make all grace abound to you, so that in all
things at all times, having all that you need,
you will abound in every good work. As it is
written: "He has scattered abroad his gifts to
the poor; his righteousness endures forever."
Now he who supplies seed to the sower and
bread for food will also supply and increase
your store of seed and will enlarge the harvest
of your righteousness. You will be made rich in
every way so that you can be generous on every
occasion, and through us your generosity will
result in thanksgiving to God.*

God will bless the giver. It is a natural outflow
and result of being generous. In fact, if you are part
of a Christian ministry, ask your best donors and
they will testify how God has richly blessed them as
they have been able to give generously to your work.
It may not be that their wealth has increased, but
they will tell you they have received intangibles of
spiritual blessings that can only come through giving.

I believe in our day and age… especially within the capitalist societies of the western world… it's tough to come into alignment with God's view of giving. But it must be a priority. It is our call and responsibility as leaders to challenge the Church to liberally and generously fund God's Kingdom work by investing—with a willing heart—what God has entrusted to each of us. And it's our responsibility, as followers of Christ, to use what He has given us to empower and strengthen His Kingdom work.

That means we not only have to teach the biblical view of money and the principles of biblical giving, but we must direct and challenge Christians to give. That means we must ask!

CHAPTER FIVE

THE BIBLICAL VIEW OF ASKING

The final piece of intelligence that we need to fight the spiritual battle of funding Christian ministry is to understand how God views asking His people for money.

Let me start by reminding you that we've seen that God desires to have our whole heart… and where we put our money is where our heart is. So it's obvious that investing in God's Kingdom work is vital to Him having our whole heart.

But there's just one problem. The inclination of the human heart is to place its affection on money rather than on God. Take a look at 1 Timothy 6:9-10 and 6:17-19,

> *People who want to get rich fall into temptation and a trap and into many foolish and harmful desires that plunge men into ruin and destruction. For the love of money is a root of all*

71

*kinds of evil. Some people, eager for money, have
wandered from the faith and pierced themselves
with many griefs.*

*Command those who are rich in this present
world not to be arrogant nor to put their hope
in wealth, which is so uncertain, but to put
their hope in God, who richly provides us with
everything for our enjoyment. Command them
to do good, to be rich in good
deeds, and to be generous and
willing to share. In this way
they will lay up treasure for
themselves as a firm foundation
for the coming age, so that they
may take hold of the life that is
truly life.*

THE PROBLEM
BEGINS WHEN WE
ERRONEOUSLY
PLACE OUR
AFFECTION ON
MONEY.

Paul took the time to give Timothy instructions
regarding wealth and money because he knew it is
human nature for us to misplace our affection on
money. In fact, in this passage Paul shows us there
are three natural inclinations we must battle:

- the inclination to love money,
- the inclination to use money to boost our ego, and
- the inclination for money to become the source of our security.

The problem begins when we erroneously place our affection on money. We've already seen the warning Solomon gives us in Ecclesiastes 3 as he tested life to see what would truly satisfy. Money will never satisfy.

But loving money is a natural bent of the heart. And it is a dangerous spiritual bent. Because when our hearts love money, they will be moved away from God. Put another way, God cannot have our whole heart if money has captured the affection of our heart.

Money will end up occupying the place in our heart that God should occupy.

God's Appointed Role for Leaders

So what does God do? Knowing that it's our

natural inclination to place our affection on money, He uses His appointed leaders, as Paul charged Timothy, to challenge His people to invest in His Kingdom program. Because God knows when His people do invest in His work, their hearts will be His.

The first recorded instance of God mandating a leader to challenge His people to give can be found in the passage we looked at earlier in Exodus 25. You will recall that God told Moses the following in this passage:

> *"Tell the Israelites to bring me an offering. You are to receive the offering for me from each man whose heart prompts him to give" (v. 2).*

Interesting. God mandates a fundraising event! He mandates that Moses, the leader of God's people, ask the people to give. I wonder what the gentleman who wrote that letter criticizing fundraising would say to God about this!

In Exodus 35:4-5, Moses obeys God's command

and tells the sons of Israel,

> *"This is what the LORD has commanded:*
> *From what you have, take an offering for the*
> *LORD. Everyone who is willing is to bring to the*
> *LORD an offering of gold, silver, and bronze...."*

Notice that Moses recognized that this was God's command (not just a suggestion!), and we have the first recorded fundraising campaign.

GOD EXPECTS HIS PEOPLE TO GIVE TO HIS KINGDOM WORK... AND HE EXPECTS LEADERS TO CHALLENGE AND DIRECT THEM WHERE TO GIVE.

In this one event, I believe God establishes a precedent that is timeless:

God expects His people to give to His Kingdom work... and He expects leaders to challenge and direct them where to give.

This is precisely the instruction Paul gave Timothy in 1 Timothy 6. In this passage, Paul charges Timothy to challenge believers to be generous with their wealth. He is, in fact, instructing Timothy to command God's people to give to God's purposes.

Back in 1 Chronicles 29, God moves through David in the same way… to challenge the people of Israel to give generously to the building of the temple. Here is what David said,

> *Then King David said to the whole assembly: "My son Solomon, the one whom God has chosen, is young and inexperienced. The task is great, because this palatial structure is not for man but for the LORD God. With all my resources I have provided for the temple of my God—gold for the gold work, silver for the silver, bronze for the bronze, iron for the iron and wood for the wood, as well as onyx for the settings, turquoise, stones of various colors, and all kinds of fine stone and marble—all of these in large quantities. Besides, in my devotion to the temple of my God I now give my personal treasures of gold and silver for the temple of my God, over and above everything I have provided for this*

holy temple: three thousand talents of gold (gold of Ophir) and seven thousand talents of refined silver, for the overlaying of the walls of the buildings, for the gold work and the silver work, and for all the work to be done by the craftsmen. Now, who is willing to consecrate himself today to the LORD?"

Then the leaders of families, the officers of the tribes of Israel, the commanders of thousands and commanders of hundreds, and the officials in charge of the king's work gave willingly. They gave toward the work on the temple of God five thousand talents and ten thousand darics of gold, ten thousand talents of silver, eighteen thousand talents of bronze and a hundred thousand talents of iron. Any who had precious stones gave them to the treasury of the temple of the LORD in the custody of Jehiel the Gershonite. The people rejoiced at the willing response of their leaders, for they had given freely and wholeheartedly to the LORD. David the king also rejoiced greatly.

David boldly stood before the people and made his case as to why they should give to the building of the temple. He challenged them directly when he asked, "Who is willing to consecrate himself today to the LORD?" And when he did, the result was spectacular!

THE PEOPLE CONSECRATED THEMSELVES TO GOD AND THEY EXPRESSED THAT CONSECRATION THROUGH GIVING OUTRAGEOUSLY.

The people consecrated themselves to God and they expressed that consecration through giving outrageously. Read the following words from 1 Chronicles 29:17-18 carefully,

> *"I know, my God, that **you test the heart** and are pleased with **integrity**. All these things have I given willingly and with honest intent. And now I have seen with joy how willingly your people who are here have given to you. O LORD, God of our fathers Abraham, Isaac and Israel, keep this **desire in the hearts of your people forever**, and **keep their hearts loyal to you**"* *(emphasis added)*.

David knew that properly motivated giving came from the willing heart of God's people. And such giving resulted in the people's hearts being directed to God Himself. So when the people of Israel gave so generously to God's Kingdom work, God really got what He wanted—the whole heart of His people.

Over and over we have seen that proper giving comes from a willing heart. The willing heart is a heart that sees the importance of giving to God's Kingdom purpose and happily does so. It is giving that comes from a heart that is clearly aligned with God's Kingdom purposes.

When God's people give willingly, it makes them prone to give even more as their hearts are given to God and His work with abandon!

Now, the question I'd like to pose to you is this: *If God's people aren't challenged or directed where to give, how in the world are they going to know where to give? Or why to give?*

The gentleman whose letter I quoted at the

beginning of this book wouldn't know where or why to give. He basically said, "If it's God's thing, then God will provide the money for you." While it is true that God will raise the money, He most often does so after we make the need known... and He will only do it through His people.

This kind of challenge is precisely the kind of challenge Paul gives the Corinthian church. Let's look at 2 Corinthians 8:1-6 again from this light,

> *And now brothers, we want you to know about the grace that God has given in the Macedonian churches. Out of the most severe trial, their **overflowing** joy and their **extreme** poverty **welled up** in **rich generosity**. For I testify that they gave as much as they were able, and even **beyond** their ability. Entirely on their own, they urgently **pleaded with** us for the privilege of sharing in this service to the saints. And they did not do as we expected, but they gave themselves **first** to the Lord and then to us in keeping with God's will. So we urged Titus,*

*since he had earlier made a beginning, to bring
also to completion this act of grace on your part
(emphasis added).*

As we've already mentioned, Paul gets in the face of the Corinthians all throughout the eighth and ninth chapters of 2 Corinthians. They had made a commitment to support God's people in Jerusalem, but it was a commitment they were not honoring. God fully expected them to honor that commitment and He had used

THE NORM FOR MOVING THE CHURCH TO FUND GOD'S WORK IS LEADERSHIP BEING WILLING TO STEP TO THE FRONT AND ISSUE THE CHALLENGE.

Paul to motivate both the Macedonian church and the Corinthian church to support the needs of the saints in Jerusalem—where God was at work.

So the norm for moving the Church to fund God's work is leadership being willing to step to the front and issue the challenge. It's often the only way most people will know where to give.

Can God work miracles? Absolutely. Does God touch the hearts of His people involved in ministry without someone ever contacting them? Sure. Is that the norm? No! Most people give to specific organizations in response to the challenges the leaders of those organizations set before them. That's why God has made it the responsibility of leadership to ask people to give.

Motivating God's People to Give Brings Honor to God

When people give as the result of being properly challenged, it truly honors God. Just take a look at the entire passage of 1 Chronicles 29:10-20. If you've never read this whole passage before, you might want to bookmark it and come back to it later. It's a wonderful prayer that David offers in praise to God for the response of the nation of Israel to the challenge he had issued.

In 2 Corinthians 9:10-11, Paul echoes how such

giving truly honors God. He writes,

> *Now he who supplies seed to the sower and bread for food will also supply and increase your store of seed and will enlarge the harvest of your righteousness. You will be made rich in every way so that you can be generous on every occasion, and through us your generosity will result in thanksgiving to God.*

Loosely translated, this passage suggests that when people give (because they are being properly challenged), it results in praise and thanksgiving to God. Why? First of all, it demonstrates that the giver recognizes God's sovereignty. Second, the giver recognizes what has been given has really come from God's hand. And third, the giver has given more than his or her money... he or she has given God what He really wants, his or her heart.

So my challenge to you today, if you are a Christian leader, is to actively and willingly take on the responsibility of asking God's people to support God's work through your church or organization.

After all, it's not about you, but about the funding of His Kingdom purposes as He uses your church or organization to shine the light of His truth into our spiritually dark world.

A Final Thought

So what is biblical fundraising all about? At its core, it's two things.

First, it's raising the funds to ensure God's Kingdom work here on earth receives the financing it needs to move forward. And, second, it is aligning the heart of God's people with God's Kingdom program. To make God's passion the passion of the Church. To have the Christian treasure what God treasures.

But there are powerful forces of evil actively engaged in undermining God's work in the world today. They and we are locked in an epic spiritual struggle with the hearts of men, women, and children as the prize. And a major front in that battle is the funding of God's work here on earth.

Satan desires to see God's work limited by the lack of financial support. When funding is limited because we fail to engage God's people to support God's work, it means two things: The impact of God's work is marginalized… to the devil's great delight… and the hearts of God's people are not fully given to God and the passion of His heart.

It's no wonder God established the precedent in Exodus 25 of His children funding His Kingdom work!

As leaders of God's people, we should embrace this calling of fundraising with great fervor and excitement as we understand all that is at stake. In fact, I believe we should make fundraising a priority, not only for what it can do to advance our ministry, although that is crucial, but because of what it accomplishes for God—aligning the heart of God's people with God's heart.

So how do you do that? Let me give you three principles from which to build your fundraising program in a way that will fulfill God's mandate.

Clearly Direct People Where to Give

People need you to provide clear, specific examples of how God is at work in your church or organization along with the related financial need so they can understand where and how best to invest in God's work through your ministry. Notice that in each biblical example of fundraising (Exodus 35, 1 Chronicles 29, 2 Corinthians 8-9), God's people were asked to give to something very specific. The purpose of their giving was to support God's work in the world at that moment in time.

This is a part of your responsibility as well—to direct God's people where to invest in God's work so they will see the impact of their giving for the Kingdom… and their hearts will be aligned with God's heart.

Be Willing to Challenge People to Give to the Work God is Doing Through Your Ministry

I often wonder if Christian leaders really believe the work of their ministry is part of what God is doing in the world today. Why? Because they are so hesitant to ask people to financially support the ministry they lead.

There's no better use of one's money than investing it in what God is doing in our world. So it makes sense that if we truly believe God has raised up our church or organization to accomplish His Kingdom purpose, we should have the boldness as leaders to challenge God's people to put their money into His work… like Moses, David, and Paul did.

One of the things Christian leaders must get over is the embarrassment they feel when they ask for money. Most often, that embarrassment is caused by a feeling that they are asking for themselves. No, you are inviting other believers to join in the greatest cause on earth—the advancement of God's Kingdom! That should lead to a boldness and passion to see people give generously to the ministry God has called you to lead.

By the way, there will always be slackers like the Corinthian church. There will always be those who complain because "you ask too much." But their response is not our responsibility! In fact, I believe their response says more about them than about you and your ministry.

As leaders, we are responsible to challenge God's people to give, and as God's people are properly challenged, it is their responsibility to give.

Show Donors the Impact
of Their Gifts in People's Lives

Once people do support the work of your church or organization, show them how their gifts are being used by God through your ministry to change people's lives. And do so on a regular basis.

One of the things I come across quite often is the reluctance of ministries to communicate frequently with their donors. There is an underlying belief that monthly communication will irritate people.

One ministry I began working with in the UK in 1997 thought this way and only mailed to their donors four times a year. I was told the donors would reduce their support if the organization mailed more frequently. But I challenged them to think about those communications as a way to build a long-term relationship with their donors.

After a decade of working together, we now mail to their donors 11 times a year, with greater response than ever and many times more the funding! In fact, in a recent survey these donors overwhelmingly affirmed the amount of mail they were receiving.

I work around the globe in a variety of cultures and countries. And one thing that is true of every culture is that God has created all of us as relational beings. And you can't build a relationship with someone without communicating with them!

What your donors don't want is irrelevant communication. What your donors do want to hear is how their support is making a difference. And they want to know how they can continue to invest in your work most effectively. You can't do either of those without communicating with some level of frequency.

Communicating with your donors can

be done in a variety of ways. While there are specifics you will need to deal with to develop the right message through the proper medium, frequent communication should be a priority for you and your ministry.

If you can develop relevant, frequent communication with your donors, you will help your supporters understand the "return" they are receiving on their investment in your ministry. You will answer the question of how effective they have been as stewards of God's money. And most importantly, you will help align their hearts with the heart of God as He works to reach lives in the world through your ministry.

✛

So my challenge to you today is to, first of all, understand that the funding of your ministry is one of the key battlefronts in the intense spiritual war raging all around us. If your ministry is going to have the impact God intends, it's pivotal to engage His people in the work He is doing in the world today.

With that understanding, embrace your God-given responsibility to challenge God's people to support God's work with fervor. As you do, trust that it will achieve God's greatest desire—to win the hearts of people… and to secure the whole-hearted devotion of each of His children.

Dunham+Company

15455 Dallas Parkway, Sixth Floor
Addison, TX 75001
USA
(972) 764-3516
dunhamandcompany.com

2 Leabons Lane
Seven Hills NSW 2147
Australia
+61 (2) 8811 5599
dunhamandcompany.com.au